SRA Early Interventions in Re

D0864584

Stuck in the Snow

By
Hilary Mac Austin

Illustrated by
Angela Adams

Columbus, OH

The McGraw·Hill Companies

SRAonline.com

 SRA

Contents

Chapter 1

Going to the Canyon 1

Chapter 2

The Storm Hits 9

Chapter 3

Be Prepared 19

Chapter 4

Dinner in the Car 29

Chapter 5

Saved! 36

Chapter 1
Going to the Canyon

Nikki Sutherly is excited, and her younger brother Alexander is too. The Sutherly children are on their first trip ever! It's spring break, and they're on a camping trip. They've been driving for a few days and playing games, and today they will ultimately arrive at the campsite.

The Sutherlys are going to camp near the Grand Canyon. Nikki is ten, and she wants to be a famous scientist when she grows up. Her favorite class in school is earth science. Alexander is eight and wants to be a firefighter—just like his mom and dad.

The Sutherlys are almost at the Grand Canyon. They're driving up the steepest mountain roads they've ever seen. On one side of the road are vertical cliffs dropping into huge canyons. Nikki can see for miles. The blue sky is enormous, but there are dark clouds gathering on the horizon.

Dad looks uneasily at the threatening clouds. "We should find out about the weather," he says. He turns on the radio and finds a weather report.

"Hey, folks," says the weather reporter cheerily, "it seems an unexpected storm is moving in from the north. Welcome to spring in northern Arizona!"

Nikki and Alexander are ecstatic. They've never seen snow before. Alexander bounces on the backseat, and Mom and Dad glance at each other. "Do you think we should turn around?" asks Mom.

"Well, we're more than halfway there. It will take longer if we turn and go back," Dad says softly.

He looks in the rearview mirror and in a louder voice says, "Anyway, it's only twenty more miles. We'll be there in no time."

Alexander and Nikki whoop with happiness. Snow *and* the Grand Canyon! Life is fantastic! Nikki looks out the window again, but something seems different.

The shadowy clouds have moved fast, and now they're covering the sun. Only a few minutes ago it was the loveliest sunny spring day, and now everything seems gray and cold. It starts snowing, and Nikki and Alexander gasp. The snowflakes look like feathers tumbling slowly from the sky.

Dad drives more carefully, but soon the road becomes flatter, and they enter a forest. Mom and Dad sigh with relief. They didn't like driving up a mountain in the slippery snow. Nikki doesn't notice—she can't stop staring out the window. "It's so unbelievably beautiful," she whispers.

Chapter 2
The Storm Hits

The gentle snowfall doesn't last long, however. Soon the snowflakes get smaller and fall faster, and the wind begins to blow violently. Dad turns on the headlights, and then the weather reporter comes on again. "Hey, there, folks," he reports, "our innocent spring snowstorm has turned into a real blizzard!"

"You know the rules," he continues. "Get off the road, and get inside. We're getting reports of winds up to . . ." The voice begins to crackle. Soon all they can hear is static. The signal is gone! Mom and Dad look at each other unsmilingly. They're worried. This is serious!

"We'll be okay," Dad says quietly to Mom. She nods and tries to relax. Dad drives slowly, and his face is tense. The car is barely moving as Dad attempts to see where he's going, but all he can see are millions of tiny white snowflakes blustering everywhere!

Dad has to stop the car. He can't continue driving because he can't see the road anymore! Everyone remains quiet. Mom looks at Dad and at Nikki and Alexander. Then Mom smiles and claps her hands rapidly. "Well, it looks like we're camping in the car tonight!" she says.

Dad grins back at Mom. "Sure looks like it," he says. "Aw, this'll be no problem," he adds, looking at Nikki and Alexander. "We're tough firefighters, aren't we?" Dad always says this when he wants Nikki and Alexander to be brave. Nikki wants to be brave, but suddenly she's terrified.

The wind is howling, and Nikki feels cold, small, and unhappy. *How can everyone be so calm?* she thinks as she tries not to cry.

"We have our camping gear," Mom says.

"And you packed enough food for an army," adds Dad.

"And *I* have my adventure kit!" says Alexander proudly.

Mom, Dad, and Nikki all look at Alexander with curiosity. "Your what?" asks Dad.

"My adventure kit," Alexander says happily. "In case we had an adventure." Alexander starts rummaging through his backpack. He removes a compass, a flashlight, batteries, rope, garbage bags, candles, a bright orange scarf, and beef jerky.

"Honey, your adventure kit is going to be such a gigantic help," says Mom.

Nikki feels a little jealous. *Alexander is helping with his silly adventure kit, and he's the youngest. I should be helping too,* she thinks. But she's too frightened to think. She can't remember anything!

"Okay, guys, this car is becoming colder. I think we need to unpack our supplies from the trunk. I'll get them," says Dad.

"I'll help," agrees Mom.

Nikki imagines her parents in the enormous storm and then suddenly remembers something: She has learned about blizzards! How could she forget?

"No! Wait!" shouts Nikki. "Listen, everyone! I know about blizzards. We studied them in school." Everyone stops and looks seriously at her.

"Go on, baby," says Mom slowly.

"Well, the air becomes frigid, and the wind blows really violently," Nikki says quickly. "It's easy to become lost or get frostbite."

Chapter 3
Be Prepared

Nikki is thinking fast now. "First, we need Alexander's rope," she says. "That way, one person can hold on to the other person." They decide Dad will go out and Mom will hold the rope.

"First, Dad, you need to rewrap yourself with more clothes," says Nikki. "It could be below zero outside!"

"Dad, don't go outside!" Alexander cries suddenly. He looks at everyone with wide eyes.

Nikki understands being scared. "It'll be okay, Alexander," she says.

Mom reassures him in her gentlest voice. "These are just adventure rules."

"He'll be safe?" asks Alexander.

"Sure I will!" Dad says confidently. "I promise. Now, hand over your socks, little man!"

Alexander regains his smile, and soon everyone has offered a piece of their clothing.

"Pretty good, Dad," says Nikki, "but you need something to keep you dry in that wet snow. I know! Alexander, we need your garbage bags."

Alexander smiles even wider. "Oh, and here's the flashlight, Dad. You'll need that too," he says proudly.

Then Nikki leans toward the front seat.

"I don't want to frighten Alexander again," she whispers to her parents, "but during our blizzard review, we learned that a blizzard's snow can bury a car. People will be unable to discover us. We need to tie something to the antenna—it's the highest part of the car. People will see it."

"Nikki, I'm so delighted you pay attention in school," Mom whispers back. Then Mom says loudly, "Because this is a real adventure, I think we need a flag. Do you have something in your adventure kit, Alexander?"

"My orange scarf! It'll be a perfect adventure flag!" Alexander says with enthusiasm. The scarf reappears in his hand.

Soon Dad is ready to go. He has Mom's red sweatshirt tied around his neck, Nikki's yellow sweater covering his head and ears, Alexander's socks as mittens, one of Alexander's garbage bags as a raincoat, and the other bags tied over his galoshes. The rope is retied around his waist again and again.

Alexander giggles. "You look absolutely ridiculous, Dad."

"He does, doesn't he?" says Mom, chuckling. "Hold on, I need to find a camera. Your friends at the firehouse will love this!"

"Oh no, you don't." Dad laughs as he grabs Alexander's flashlight and scarf from the backseat and then returns to the front. "I'll never hear the end of it."

"I'll return," Dad says confidently, and then he pushes and pushes on the door. He almost can't open it because the snow is already so unbelievably high! Also, the wind is extremely strong. When he finally gets out of the car, he vanishes into the snow. Mom holds the rope tightly.

Wet snow and freezing air blow through the open door. Dad slowly pushes through the snow and wind, and Mom feeds out the rope. Then Nikki feels the trunk open and close. When Dad returns, he throws sleeping bags and backpacks into the car.

"One more trip," he gasps.

Again Dad vanishes. Mom refeeds the rope, and Nikki feels the trunk open and close. Finally Dad plunks a cooler and a shovel into the car, and then he awkwardly climbs in and shuts the door. He's covered in so much snow! He looks like a friendly snowman with outrageous clothing.

Chapter 4
Dinner in the Car

"Grab the shovel, Alexander," Mom orders. "Nikki, grab this cooler. Okay, time for a little heat." She turns on the car, unties the rope, and rips the wet garbage bags off Dad. Nikki has never seen anyone move quite so fast, but Mom is so calm and reassured! Everyone watches.

"Nikki, toss me a sleeping bag," says Mom. Then she rubs Dad's feet and hands. "Wiggle your toes, Nate," she says to Dad.

Dad envelops himself in a sleeping bag. The car is quickly getting much warmer, and the crystal snow melts off Dad's face. "Wow," he says, "that was really amazing!"

"Okay, kids," Dad says, "what do you think we should do now?"

Alexander and Nikki talk at the same time. "We should put on all our clothes," says Nikki, while Alexander shouts, "I'm hungry!"

Mom laughs merrily. "Both are very good ideas, but let's put on some more clothes first."

The Sutherlys put on all their clothes and crawl into their sleeping bags. They look quite cozy.

"Alexander, I believe we need your adventure kit again," Mom says. "We'll need the light from your candles when Dad turns off the car."

"Candles also will help keep the car from getting too uncomfortably cold," adds Nikki.

"But, Mom, what are we going to put the candles into?" asks Alexander.

"I know!" says Nikki. "Mom, do you have any empty cups?"

"Fantastic idea, Nikki," says Mom. "I have our metal camping cups somewhere." Soon the candles are safely lit, and there is the prettiest flickering light in the car.

"Okay, everyone, get ready because I'm turning off the car. We need to save the gasoline," says Dad.

Then Mom starts to open her window!

"*No!*" cry Alexander and Nikki. "It's too cold, Mom!"

"I know it's cold," says Mom. "But candles burn oxygen, and we need fresh air."

"Now, who wants dinner?" says Mom.

"I do!" Alexander and Nikki holler happily from inside their sleeping bags.

Mom makes sandwiches, Alexander gives everyone some of his beef jerky, and they drink apple juice from the cooler. It feels satisfying to be full of food, but everyone is now freezing.

Chapter 5
Saved!

"I think we need to warm up a little bit," Dad says.

Whew, Dad is going to turn on the heat! thinks Nikki.

But instead Dad says, "Come on, everybody, let's get moving! Wiggle your bodies!" He starts singing. Soon they're all singing and wiggling in their sleeping bags.

The dancing and singing work. Everyone is warmer, and Mom blows out the candles and closes the window a bit. "Bedtime," she says. Nikki and Alexander snuggle in their sleeping bags and soon are sleeping soundly. Mom and Dad stay awake all night to make sure their children remain safe and unhurt.

The next morning Nikki is startled by a loud noise. Dad is honking the horn! Nikki pops her head out of the sleeping bag. Sunshine is pouring into the car through the tops of the windows. The car is nearly covered by the unrelenting snow.

Why is Dad honking? she wonders curiously.

She hears yelling from outside. Hooray! Help has arrived! Nikki is unbelievably happy. She shakes Alexander. Suddenly she hears someone walking on the roof of the car. Then she sees feet walking next to the top of Mom's window! The feet are walking on top of the snow! The person leans over.

The friendly face of a park ranger appears in Mom's window.

"Well, look what we have here," the ranger says. "Is everyone okay?"

"Are we glad to see you!" says Mom with relief. "We're all fine, but we'd love to get out of this car!"

The ranger laughs. "I can understand that!"

The ranger shovels snow away from Mom's window. Soon the window can open all the way. One by one, the Sutherlys crawl out the window and stand in the bright sunshine. Alexander plays and falls in the deep snow. Nikki just stares at the bright white blanket of snow everywhere.

The ranger looks at the sky. "This storm caught everyone by surprise. We've been digging out people all morning. I almost missed you, but I saw the scarf on your antenna and returned. And you kept a window open. Both are really intelligent moves. You really know your blizzard survival rules."

"We've never seen snow before," says Dad. He points to Alexander and Nikki and adds, "Our kids were unafraid and had all the answers."

"We used my adventure kit!" says Alexander happily.

"Wow, I've never heard of an adventure kit," says the ranger. "You'll have to tell me everything about it."

The ranger carries Alexander to her snowmobile. Alexander chatters the entire way, telling and retelling the ranger all about his adventure kit. The ranger nods and smiles at the small boy. Mom and Dad give Nikki a hug.

"I'm so proud of you," Mom whispers into Nikki's ear. "You saved our lives!"